Let's Roll
DRAGSTERS

by Wendy Hinote Lanier

FOCUS
READERS

North Star
EDITIONS

www.northstareditions.com

Produced for North Star Editions by Red Line Editorial.

Photographs ©: Jeff Speer/Icon Sportswire/AP Images, cover, 1; Juerg Schreiter/Shutterstock Images, 4–5; Sam Sefton/iStockphoto, 7; Action Sports Photography/Shutterstock Images, 9, 18; AP Images, 10–11, 12; Michael Stokes/ Shutterstock Images, 14, 29; Phillip Rubino/Shutterstock Images, 16–17, 22–23; Mike Brake/Shutterstock Images, 20; Manfred Steinbach/Shutterstock Images, 25; Steve Mann/Shutterstock Images, 26–27

ISBN
978-1-63517-048-1 (hardcover)
978-1-63517-104-4 (paperback)
978-1-63517-205-8 (ebook pdf)
978-1-63517-155-6 (hosted ebook)

Library of Congress Control Number: 2016951020

Printed in the United States of America
Mankato, MN
November, 2016

About the Author

Wendy Hinote Lanier is a native Texan and former elementary teacher who writes and speaks to children and adults on a variety of topics. She is the author of more than 20 books for children and young people. Some of her favorite people are dogs.

TABLE OF CONTENTS

CHAPTER 1

RACE TO THE FINISH

Two dragsters move to the staging area. Their tires scream as the drivers spin them on the concrete to heat the rubber. The heated rubber improves the tires' grip.

Dragster drivers spin their tires before every race.

Then the cars move to the starting line.

When both cars are staged, drivers see three amber lights. Then comes the green light. The drivers hit the accelerators. The cars speed down the strip. Four seconds later, they cross the finish line.

FUN FACT

The series of lights that start a drag race is called a Christmas tree.

 A tall set of lights tells drivers when to start.

The drivers apply the brakes and release the parachutes. The parachutes pop out in a flash of color. The drivers ease the cars off the track and onto the return road. Slowly, the drivers make their way back to the pit after stopping

ELIMINATION ROUNDS

Most drag racing events are a series of **elimination** rounds. The winner of each round advances to the next. The final race is between the two cars with the best times.

 Parachutes help drivers slow down when the race is over.

to receive their time slips. The slips tell who is going home and who will move on to the next race.

CHAPTER 2

DRAG RACING HISTORY

During World War II (1939–1945), factories were busy making vehicles for the war. There were few cars to buy. After the war, cars went back into production.

 A man waves a flag to begin a drag race in the 1950s.

 A dragster's front wheels come off the ground during a race in 1961.

The new car engines were more powerful. Car owners raced one another on dry lakebeds and two-lane roads. The races were not legal, but they became very popular.

The first organized drag races happened in 1949. In each race, two cars began from a complete stop called a standing start. The cars covered a distance of 0.25 miles (0.40 km). The goal was to reach the finish line in the fastest time. This is known as elapsed time.

FUN FACT

Police were happy when drag racing moved to drag strips. It meant races were legal, safer, and off the streets.

 Flames shoot out of a dragster's exhaust when the car accelerates.

In 1950, the first **commercial** drag strip opened. Within a year, the editor of *Hot Rod* magazine, Wally Parks, created the National Hot Rod Association (NHRA).

Today, the NHRA sets safety rules and race standards. The NHRA oversees races to make sure everyone follows the rules. It is the largest motorsports authority in the world.

TYPES OF CARS

Early drag races included all types of cars. The engine was what mattered. As drag racing grew, new rules created classes. Each class included cars of similar size, type, and weight. Today, the NHRA approves and controls more than 200 classes of cars.

CHAPTER 3

DRAGSTER BASICS

Professional drag racing has four major classes. Three of them are for cars. The fourth is for motorcycles.

The fastest drag racers in the world are the Top Fuel class.

Barbara Burt prepares for a race in her dragster.

PARTS OF A TOP FUEL DRAGSTER

airfoil

driver's seat

Top Fuel cars have large rear
wheels and small front wheels. A
large **airfoil** over the rear causes air
to press the car to the track.

In a single race, a Top Fuel car can burn up to 15 gallons (57 L) of fuel. These cars require a special fuel made with **nitromethane**.

TOP FUEL ENGINES

Top Fuel engines sit behind the driver. This became standard after Don Garlits's **transmission** exploded in a front-motored dragster in 1970. The explosion split the car in half, causing Garlits to lose part of his right foot. Garlits survived and soon designed a car with the engine in the back. Within two years, his design became the new standard for Top Fuel cars.

A Funny Car crew lifts the body to inspect the engine.

Funny Cars are much like Top Fuel cars. They use the same engines and the same fuel. But Funny Cars are not as long. They are also covered with a one-piece

fiberglass body. The body must be lifted up for drivers to climb in. This funny way to get in earned the cars their name.

Pro Stock cars look more like regular cars. They run on **high-octane** gasoline instead of nitromethane.

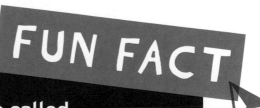

FUN FACT

Pro Stock cars are also called doorslammers because they have doors that work.

CHAPTER 4

DRAGSTERS TODAY

Today's dragsters are designed on computers. Engineers test car designs in wind tunnels. These are special tunnels where engineers study the way air flows past objects.

A Pro Stock dragster must weigh at least 2,350 pounds (1,066 kg).

Car bodies are made of lightweight steel tubing and carbon-fiber **composite**. Engines are fine-tuned to boost power and increase acceleration. And drivers work hard to improve their reaction times at the start.

FUN FACT

The NHRA Junior Drag Racing League sponsors drag racing for kids from ages 5 to 17. The kids race half-scale cars called Junior Dragsters.

 Two Top Fuel dragsters approach the starting line and prepare to race.

The fastest dragsters travel at more than 330 miles per hour (531 km/h). As technology improves, these speeds could get even faster.

DRY CLUTCHES

Top Fuel and Funny Cars do not have transmissions. A five-disc dry clutch transfers power directly from the engine to the drive wheels. The clutch is timed to gradually catch and slip as the car moves. It is tuned to match track conditions. During races, discs often get so hot that they fuse together. They must be replaced after every race.

Mechanics work on a dragster before a race.

FOCUS ON
DRAGSTERS

Write your answers on a separate piece of paper.

1. Write a sentence that describes the key ideas from Chapter 2 of this book.

2. Which type of dragster would you want to race? Why?

3. Which dragsters run on high-octane gasoline?

    A. Top Fuel

    B. Funny Cars

    C. Pro Stock

4. What might happen if a dragster did not have an airfoil?

    A. The dragster would not be able to go fast.

    B. The dragster would not stay on the ground.

    C. The dragster would run out of fuel more quickly.

5. What does **authority** mean in this book?

    A. a certain kind of racetrack

    B. a group that makes rules

    C. people who travel around the world

The NHRA oversees races to make sure everyone follows the rules. It is the largest motorsports **authority** in the world.

6. What does **accelerators** mean in this book?

    A. pedals that make cars go faster

    B. places where drivers race

    C. people who drive dragsters

The drivers hit the **accelerators**.
The cars speed down the strip.

Answer key on page 32.

GLOSSARY

airfoil
A surface, similar to an airplane wing, designed to help control a vehicle.

commercial
Done for the purpose of selling or doing business.

composite
Made up of different kinds of parts.

elimination
The process of removing people from a contest.

fiberglass
A lightweight material made of tiny strands of glass combined with resin to create a durable surface.

high-octane
Of a good quality so that an engine can run better.

nitromethane
A colorless, oily liquid used to power rockets and some race cars.

transmission
An enclosed set of gears for transferring force from the motor to the wheels of a vehicle.

TO LEARN MORE

BOOKS

Georgiou, Tyrone. *Funny Car Dragsters*. New York: Gareth Stevens Publishing, 2011.

Gigliotti, Jim. *Smokin' Dragsters and Funny Cars*. Berkeley Heights, NJ: Enslow Publishers, 2013.

Monnig, Alex. *Behind the Wheel of a Dragster*. Mankato, MN: The Child's World, 2016.

Von Finn, Denny. *Top Fuel Dragsters*. Minneapolis: Bellwether Media, 2010.

NOTE TO EDUCATORS

Visit **www.focusreaders.com** to find lesson plans, activities, links, and other resources related to this title.

INDEX

A
airfoil, 18

B
brakes, 8

C
computers, 23

E
elapsed time, 13

F
Funny Cars, 20, 26

G
gasoline, 21

H
Hot Rod magazine, 14

L
lights, 6

N
National Hot Rod
   Association, 14–15
nitromethane, 19, 21

P
parachutes, 8
Parks, Wally, 14
Pro Stock, 21

R
rubber, 5

S
staging area, 5

T
time slips, 9
Top Fuel, 17–20, 26

W
wind tunnels, 23
World War II, 11

Answer Key: 1. Answers will vary; **2.** Answers will vary; **3.** C; **4.** B; **5.** B; **6.** A

DATE DUE

			PRINTED IN U.S.A.